J 12–18

Full Track

D0891795

PLAY · TRACK NUMBER · CD 1 · ONLINE PART 1

CD 1 / Online Part 1 WHY IS THE P̶̶̶̶̶̶ SPECIAL?

1	**J.S. Bach**: Prelude in C major, BWV 846, from The Well-Tempered Clavier – Jenő Jandó, piano; 8.553796–97	2.17
2	**Rimsky-Korsakov, arr. Rachmaninov**: Flight of the Bumblebee, from The Tale of Tsar Sultan – Balázs Szokolay, piano; 8.550107	1.11
3	**Mendelssohn**: Songs without Words, No. 37 (Book 7, Op. 85 No. 1) in F major – Péter Nagy; 8.550316	2.50
4	**J.S. Bach**: French Suite No. 5 in G major, BWV 816: VII. Gigue – Wolfgang Rübsam, piano; 8.550710	3.34
5	**Joplin**: The Entertainer – Alexander Peskanov, piano; 8.559114	4.38
6	**Mozart**: Piano Concerto No. 21 in C major, K. 467 ('Elvira Madigan'): III. Allegro vivace assai – Jenő Jandó, piano; Concentus Hungaricus; András Ligeti; 8.550434	6.11
7	**Avner Dorman**: Piano Concerto in A major: I. Allegro – Eliran Avni, piano; Metropolis Ensemble; Andrew Cyr; 8.559620	5.03
8	**Kapustin**: Prelude No. 17 in A flat major – Catherine Gordeladze, piano; 8.572272	1.47
9	**Debussy**: Clair de lune, from Suite bergamasque – François-Joël Thiollier; 8.555800	5.07
10	**Confrey**: Kitten on the Keys – Eteri Andjaparidze, piano; 8.559016	2.28
11	**Shostakovich**: Prelude No. 5 in D major, from 24 Preludes and Fugues, Op. 87 – Konstantin Scherbakov, piano; 8.554745–46	1.42
12	**Scarlatti**: Keyboard Sonata in F major, K. 82 – Benjamin Frith, piano; 8.554792	2.02
13	**Brahms**: Hungarian Dance No. 5 – Silke-Thora Matthies & Christian Köhn, piano; 8.553140	2.00
14	**Fauré**: Berceuse, from Dolly Suite, Op. 56 – Pierre-Alain Volondat & Patrick De Hooge, piano; 8.553638	2.19
15	**Trimble**: Buttermilk Point (Reel) – Una Hunt & Roy Holmes, pianos; 8.225059	1.56
16	**Britten**: The Plough Boy, from Folksong Arrangements, Vol. 3 'British Isles' – Roderick Williams, baritone; Iain Burnside, piano; 8.572600	1.42
17	**Saint-Saëns**: The Swan, from The Carnival of the Animals – Peter Toperczer, piano; Slovak Radio SO (cellist unknown); 8.550335	3.05
18	**Poulenc**: Trio for oboe, bassoon and piano: III. Rondo – Olivier Doise, oboe; Laurent Lefèvre, bassoon; Alexandre Tharaud, piano; 8.553611	3.15
19	**Elgar**: Piano Quintet, Op. 84: II. Adagio (extract) – Maggini String Quartet; Peter Donohoe, piano; 8.553737	2.25
20	**Cage**: The Perilous Night No. 6 – Boris Berman, piano; 8.554562	3.33
21	**Maxwell Davies**: Farewell to Stromness (extract) – Peter Maxwell Davies, piano; 8.572408	1.37
22	**Satie**: Gymnopédie No. 1 – Klara Körmendi, piano; 8.550305	2.37
23	**Chopin**: Prelude in A major, Op. 28 No. 7 – Irina Zaritzkaya, piano; 8.550225	0.53

Total: 67.18

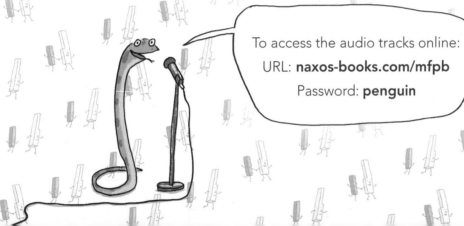

To access the audio tracks online:
URL: **naxos-books.com/mfpb**
Password: **penguin**

My First
Piano
Book

Written by **Genevieve Helsby**
Illustrated by **Jason Chapman**

The Cast

Elephant

Seagull

Horse

Pig

Snake

Duck

Published by Naxos Books,
an imprint of Naxos Rights US, Inc. © Naxos Books 2018
www.naxosbooks.com
Printed and bound in China by L.Rex

Illustration: Jason Chapman
Design and layout: Hannah Whale, Fruition – Creative Concepts
Accompaniments for Pieces 1–12 composed by Rebecca Helsby
Sound editing: Arthur Ka Wai Jenkins and K&A Productions Ltd

2

Contents

See inside front & back covers for audio track lists.

Lion

Penguin

Monkey

Frog

Tortoise

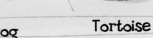

Welcome!

You can't ignore a piano.

OOPS! Sorry!

Pffft

You can't throw a
piano up in the air…

…or tread on it
by mistake.

You can't put a piano
in your suitcase
and take it on the
aeroplane.

And you certainly
can't put it in your
mouth and blow
down it…

IT'S TOO BIG!

A piano sits proudly, completely still,
waiting for someone to come and
tickle its keys…

The keys are black and white
but the sounds are full of colour!

4

This book has two parts:

1. WHY IS THE PIANO SO SPECIAL?

This is about the sound of the piano and its music.

You can listen to the tracks on CD 1
or online as you read the book.

Did you know
that the piano
can sound:

Gentle

FIERCE

Lively

FUNNY

Exciting

Peaceful

…and many other things?

Turn the pages to discover it all!

2. HOW DO I PLAY IT?

This is about learning to play the piano.

If you've never driven a car,
you can't just get behind
the wheel and zoom off.
You learn how to drive first!

Luckily you can learn the
piano as soon as you want!

Explore Part 2 and find
out how to get started.

Inside the Piano

When somebody says 'piano',
the first thing you think of is:

The keys!

Press one – and a sound comes out.

The king of pianos.

But the keys are just one part of the instrument.
Inside is a whole obstacle course…

More chance of fitting
this in your home.

Grand piano

Upright piano

There are digital pianos, too. These
are clever copy-cats. They don't need
hammers or strings. They are smaller and
cheaper. And you can use headphones
– so you can plonk in private! But a 'real'
piano, as long as it isn't too old and
tired, is a better instrument.

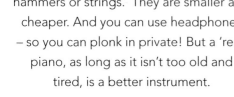

Digital piano

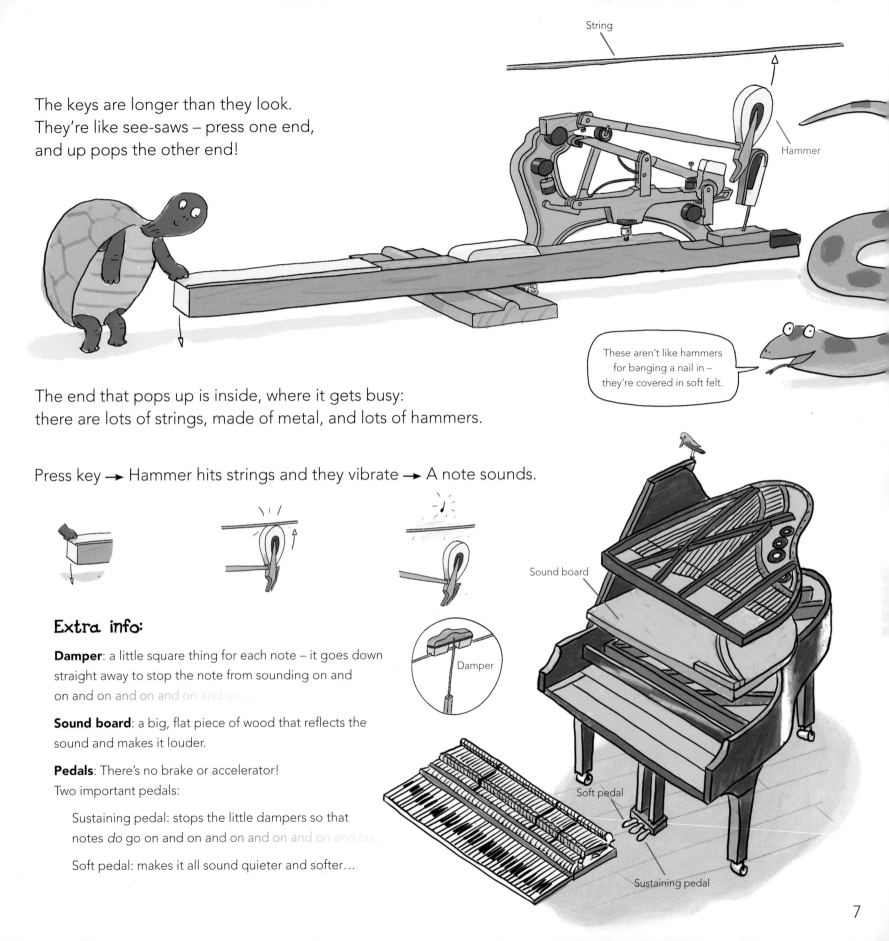

The keys are longer than they look.
They're like see-saws – press one end,
and up pops the other end!

String

Hammer

These aren't like hammers
for banging a nail in –
they're covered in soft felt.

The end that pops up is inside, where it gets busy:
there are lots of strings, made of metal, and lots of hammers.

Press key → Hammer hits strings and they vibrate → A note sounds.

Extra info:

Damper: a little square thing for each note – it goes down
straight away to stop the note from sounding on and
on and on and on and on and on…

Sound board: a big, flat piece of wood that reflects the
sound and makes it louder.

Pedals: There's no brake or accelerator!
Two important pedals:

Sustaining pedal: stops the little dampers so that
notes *do* go on and on and on and on and on and on…

Soft pedal: makes it all sound quieter and softer…

Damper

Sound board

Soft pedal

Sustaining pedal

Part 1
WHY IS THE PIANO SO SPECIAL?

A piano is a clever piece of furniture. It sits in the room like a funny-shaped table – but it's much better than that…

The piano is so complete. Some instruments can sound only one note at a time. But the piano can sound a lot of notes together. So you can play **chords** – groups of notes that go well with each other.

You can play high notes and low notes – it has a wide range of **pitch**.

The piano often 'accompanies' another instrument – maybe a violin or a flute. Its many notes can colour in the music.

An Italian inventor called Bartolomeo Cristofori made the first piano, just before 1700. After that, piano builders spent 150 years making it better and better.

Bellissimo!

9

Simple Solo

A composer is somebody who makes up music and writes it down.

300 years ago, Johann Sebastian Bach was busy with a lot of notes.

He didn't even have a piano.
Nobody had one – it was still being invented!

Instead he had a thing called a harpsichord. It was a bit like a piano but it made more of a fizzy, twinkly sound.

Today, Bach is world-famous.

Why?

Because he knew how to make a perfect piece of music.

 J.S. Bach Prelude in C major

PLAY
TRACK
1
CD 1 ONLINE PART 1

Bach wrote some very complicated things.

But even his simple music shines.

Bach was brilliant at playing the organ too – a giant instrument with keyboards, pipes and pedals. He controlled them all like a pilot in a plane!

Listen...
This music has no big crashes or fancy twiddling. It grows gently like a flower, settling peacefully at the end.

QUESTION 1
Does the music:
a. Stop and start, or
b. Keep going at the same speed?
Answer on p. 71

This piano piece starts on Middle C – the first note you will learn in section 2.

Acrobat Fingers

Have you seen how many keys there are on a full-sized piano?

88.

That's a lot to choose from!

When people get really good at the piano, their fingers can buzz around at top speed, pressing exactly the keys they want.

If you watch closely, your eyes go funny!

> Somebody who plays the piano is called a 'pianist'.

Rimsky-Korsakov Flight of the Bumblebee

PLAY
TRACK
2
CD 1 ONLINE PART 1

'Nikolai Rimsky-Korsakov' – that's not a name you hear every day. Can you say it without getting your tongue in a muddle? NICK-OH-LYE RIM-SKEE KOR-SAH-KOFF

Like his Russian name, Rimsky-Korsakov's music has crisp and colourful sounds.

Listen...

Flight of the Bumblebee is fast music. A bee flies fast. Imagine it searching for a nice flower to bury its little face in.

Rimsky-Korsakov wrote *Flight of the Bumblebee* for a whole orchestra. So 50 people on different instruments made the bumblebee fly! Here, just one person is at the piano – yet he plays the same music that the orchestra played. Isn't that amazing.

QUESTION 2

How many people are playing this piece?
a. 10, b. 50, or c. 1

Answer on p. 71

11

Singing

It is almost impossible to *sing* 'Flight of the Bumblebee'.

The voice needs a 'melody' (a tune) to sing.

We sing lullabies to babies – soothing melodies to help them sleep.

We sing along with a piano, too.

But sometimes the piano has a lovely, singing melody of its own.

The piano can play the tune *and* some nice notes underneath, making a complete song all by itself.

Hello! You're a nice note

Mendelssohn Songs without Words, No. 37 in F major

PLAY TRACK 3 CD / ONLINE PART

Felix Mendelssohn was lucky: his mother taught him to play the piano when he was six years old. He was good at it.

His parents were friends with important scientists and artists, and invited them round. Imagine coming home from school and finding a mathematical genius in your kitchen!

Felix himself became important, too.

He wrote a lot of piano pieces called 'Songs without Words' – because of course the piano can't sing words, so it makes sense not to have any!

Listen...

There are two parts: 1. The 'singing' melody or tune (in the right hand), like a boat sailing with the breeze; 2. A gentle 'accompaniment' (in the left hand), like watery waves underneath.

QUESTION 3

Is the melody in this piece:
a. At the top in the right hand, or
b. At the bottom in the left hand?

Answer on p. 71

Felix's sister, Fanny, was musical too. But when she was born, in 1805, it was hard for a girl to become a composer. People were more interested in her brother. If she had been born in our time, she might have become as famous as Felix!

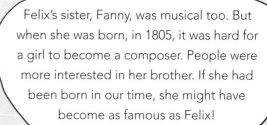

13

Dancing

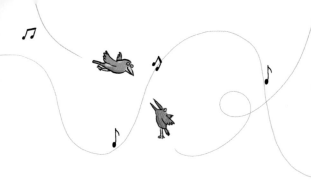

Everyone can do *some* sort of dance.
Even if you flop around like a puppet, it doesn't matter!
Dancing is moving for fun.

But nobody dances without music.

Sometimes, it's the *music* that is dancing, and you don't need to. You can just listen.

You might tap your foot without thinking about it.

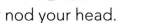

Or nod your head.

Or wiggle your bottom if you thought nobody was looking…

Dance music is all about rhythm. You can feel the beat, and that's what makes you move.

J.S. Bach French Suite No. 5: Gigue

PLAY TRACK 4 CD 1 ONLINE PART

We've heard about Johann Sebastian Bach already.
He's the one with the harpsichord and the C major Prelude.

His Gigue is more lively. It's a dance.

Listen...

The music keeps skipping along and makes *me* want to skip too! I wish I could...

QUESTION 4

Does this music sound:
a. Shy, b. Happy, or c. Grumpy?

Answer on p. 71

A suite is a set of things that belong together – like a suite of furniture. In music, a dance suite has four or five little pieces, each with a different mood.

Joplin The Entertainer

PLAY TRACK 5 CD 1 ONLINE PART

The Entertainer is a piano rag.
It doesn't clean the piano –
'ragtime' was a type of music.

Ragtime started in America before jazz, and Scott Joplin was really good at it.

Listen...

The left hand (at the bottom) is like a bouncing ball, but the right hand (with the tune) does its own thing. It's cheeky!

QUESTION 5

Does the piece end with:
a. The same tune we hear at the beginning, or
b. A different one?

Answer on p. 71

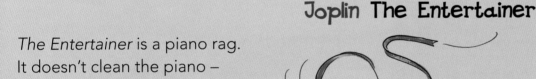

15

Playing with an Orchestra

Quiet everyone.
The orchestra is ready.
The violinists look serious.
The trumpeters look important.
The bassoonist is smiling.
Nobody coughs.

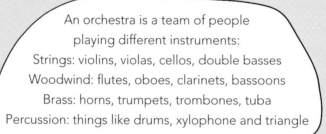

An orchestra is a team of people
playing different instruments:
Strings: violins, violas, cellos, double basses
Woodwind: flutes, oboes, clarinets, bassoons
Brass: horns, trumpets, trombones, tuba
Percussion: things like drums, xylophone and triangle

On to the stage
comes the conductor
with a wobbly smile
and a large stick.

The piano's lid is open
so the notes can fly out
to the audience.

A piano isn't a member of
the orchestra – it visits more
as a solo instrument. It goes
at the front and has the
most important part.

The conductor waves
and makes faces to tell
the orchestra exactly how
to play the music. Where a
person plays an instrument,
the conductor 'plays'
the orchestra!

Then the pianist arrives.
Lots of applause!
This star guest sits at the beautiful
grand piano, and the music begins.

Mozart Piano Concerto No. 21 (movement 3)

PLAY CD 1 ONLINE PART TRACK 6

In 1759 (a long time ago), a little boy called Wolfgang was peering over his sister's shoulder while she practised the piano.

She was seven years old and had lessons. He was three and didn't. So he copied her and starting showing off!

Mozart is like a ray of sunshine in music. He was brilliant.

Mozart made up a piece called 'A Musical Joke' – people were expecting the music to end nicely so instead he made it end with a sort of splodge. He loved being a rebel!

QUESTION 6

Between 1.15 and 1.30, the orchestra is playing quietly with the piano. Does the orchestra have:
a. Short, spiky notes, or
b. Long, smooth notes?

Answer on p. 71

Listen...

The music keeps skipping along and makes us want to skip too!

Dorman Piano Concerto in A major (movement 1)

PLAY CD 1 ONLINE PART TRACK 7

Do you like fireworks?
Here are some musical ones.
Stand back!

A concerto is a big piece for a solo instrument with an orchestra.

Listen...

The piano and the violins play fast notes exactly together. It makes an exciting sound.

The American composer Avner Dorman likes classical, pop and rock music. He uses all these styles to make an exciting musical mix.

QUESTION 7

What happens at 3.51?
a. The piano plays with no orchestra, or
b. The orchestra plays with no piano.

Answer on p. 71

Getting Jazzy

Imagine you start telling a story, but you make it up as you go along.

You're not reading the words from a book: they're coming straight from your head and out of your mouth. So you are free to make the story go however you want.

In music or drama, there's a name for making things up as you go along: it's called 'improvisation'. Mostly you do it on purpose. Sometimes you do it because you forget what's meant to come next...

Jazz music is like that.
Often the musicians make up the music as they go along.
They feel free.

Rhythm is important in jazz. The music has complicated beats and fun patterns.

The piano is a great jazz instrument.

Time to find your sunglasses and look cool.

Kapustin Prelude No. 17

PLAY · TRACK 8 · CD 1 ONLINE PART 1

School's finished!
The doors are open and you're free to go.
This is Friday music.
The weekend is coming – no lessons.

Listen...

Listen to the left hand – the bottom of the music – it has a kind of happy thump.

QUESTION 8

Is this music:
a. Easy to sing, or
b. Difficult to sing?

Answer on p. 71

A bouncy beat and colourful notes...
the piano is let loose too!

Good pianists can play without looking at their hands. They just know where all the notes are.

19

Painting a Picture

Music is powerful.
It has the power to drive your imagination.
So it can make you see a picture in your head.

Sometimes the picture is exactly
what the composer wanted you to
see when he or she wrote the music.

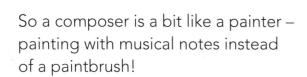

So a composer is a bit like a painter –
painting with musical notes instead
of a paintbrush!

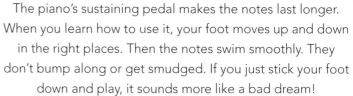

The piano's sustaining pedal makes the notes last longer.
When you learn how to use it, your foot moves up and down
in the right places. Then the notes swim smoothly. They
don't bump along or get smudged. If you just stick your foot
down and play, it sounds more like a bad dream!

Debussy Clair de lune (Moonlight)

PLAY
TRACK
9
CD 1 ONLINE PART 1

Moonlight is magical.

When the sky is clear and the moon is big and bright, you can see everything, even though it's dark!

It's strange because there's no colour. And somehow it is peaceful...
...as if the world has stopped.

Listen...

Imagine it's midnight. It's frosty. All is calm. Everyone is asleep. Outside, the moonlight is shining across the fields and the grass is glowing.

QUESTION 9

The piano's sustaining pedal makes notes longer and music smoother. Do you think the pedal is used in this piece?
a. Yes, or b. No.

Answer on p. 71

Clair de lune uses most of the piano's keyboard – you can hear some very low notes and some very high ones too.

Clair de lune is French for 'Moonlight'.

Describing Something

Moonlight can't last for ever…
everyone wakes up in the morning.

People are shouting, the dog wants a walk,
maybe someone burnt the toast. The world is alive!

The piano can describe these things, too.

It doesn't dress up.
It doesn't have a screen.
It can't speak.

So how does it do it?

It's all about how its keys are pressed.

Key is pressed **slowly** → the sound is **quiet**.
Key is pressed **quickly** → the sound is **loud**.
Key is pressed **slowly and held down** for a long time → the sound is **still**.
Key is pressed **quickly and let up** straight away → the sound is **sudden**.
Keys are pressed **quickly one after the other** → the sound is **loud and busy**.

Imagine you're a composer. Your new piece is about a racing car.
Should you tell the pianist to press the keys slowly and hold them
down for ages? No – not unless the car has broken down!

Confrey Kitten on the Keys

Track 2 had a bumblebee on it.
The music was fast, and it didn't stop until the end.
Here's another animal. It can't fly, but it *can* jump up on the furniture…

Listen…

The little kitten is bouncing about on the piano keys, enjoying the noises!

QUESTION 10

The music is describing the kitten's paws landing all over the keyboard. Is it:
a. Smooth, b. Peaceful, or c. Bouncy?

Answer on p. 71

Zez Confrey, the composer, went to stay with his grandma. In the middle of the night, he heard strange sounds. What were they? He got out of bed… and found a cat on the piano, walking up and down the keys! He thought it was so funny that he wrote a piece of music about it, making the cat a more lively kitten!

23

Just Music

Music doesn't *have* to be about anything at all.
It can be just music.

Horse is learning a new piano piece.
This is what it's about:

Nothing!

Music that is 'just music' can still make you think of something when you listen. Maybe no one else in the world sees what you see. Your imagination is wonderful and belongs only to you.

Horse thinks his new piece is really good.
That's why he's concentrating hard,
which almost never happens.

He'd like you to hear it…

Shostakovich Prelude No. 5

This pretty piece doesn't describe a kitten or try to paint the moon.
It is called simply 'Prelude No. 5'.

PLAY TRACK 11 CD 1 ONLINE PART 1

Listen...
There are little twists and turns that you don't expect – at 0.17 the music reaches up higher, like someone exploring in the woods.

QUESTION 11
What does the music make you think of?
Answer on p. 71

This has the same name as Bach's music on track 1: Prelude. Both pieces are gentle and delicate, like beautiful ornaments on a shelf.

Scarlatti Keyboard Sonata, K. 82

Scarlatti wrote 550 pieces all called 'Keyboard Sonata'!
He didn't need to give them fancy names – we like them just as they are.

PLAY TRACK 12 CD 1 ONLINE PART 1

Listen...
At the start there are three notes, each played three times: **Da**-da-da, **Da**-da-da, **Da**-da-da. At 0:07, it happens again – with some twiddling above. At 0.13, the music is even busier but underneath you can hear it: **Da**-da-da, **Da**-da-da, **Da**-da-da. That is called a **theme**. It keeps coming in the music, and we soon listen out for it like a friend.

Scarlatti was from Italy. He died a long time before Shostakovich came along.

QUESTION 12
Which piece is slower:
a. Shostakovich's Prelude, or
b. Scarlatti's Keyboard Sonata?
Answer on p. 71

25

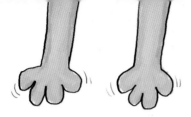

Four Hands

(or two paws and two wings)

On your computer, you only press one key at a time.
Otherwise you get this sort of thing: fhduspigh thw f bhung dfh hd

A piano is different. We can play **chords** – groups of notes that go together well. We use a different finger for each note, and put them all down at the same time.

The sound blooms when you play chords.

If you want to make it bloom even more, you need more fingers on the keys!

Two people can sit next to each other at the piano and play a **duet**.

The piano is the only instrument that is played by two people at once.

In a duet, the person playing the lower notes at the bottom of the keyboard is the one who presses the pedal.

It can be hard for two people to press keys down at exactly the same time. Sometimes it goes 'Ba-DUM' when it should have gone just 'DUM'.

There are four hands, so more notes can sound at once. And the two pianists have fun playing together.

Brahms Hungarian Dance No. 5

 PLAY TRACK **13** CD 1 ONLINE PART 1

Johannes Brahms wanted his music to be perfect.

If he composed a piece and didn't think it was good enough, he tore it up and threw it away.

Luckily his *Hungarian Dances* stayed out of the dustbin!

QUESTION 13

What happens at 1.26?
a. It slows down,
b. A trumpet joins in,
or c. The main tune comes back.

Answer on p. 71

Listen...

You can hear low notes as well as ones that twinkle at the top – four hands can cover the whole keyboard.

Fauré Berceuse from 'Dolly Suite'

 PLAY TRACK **14** CD 1 ONLINE PART 1

Fauré wrote some piano duets for a little girl called Dolly. 'Berceuse' was for Dolly's birthday: she was 1.

Listen...

Imagine the two pianists sitting next to each other, smiling as they knit together this lovely lullaby.

'Berceuse' is French for 'lullaby'.

QUESTION 14

Who do you think is playing the tune?
a. The person sitting at the top of the keyboard (the right-hand side), or
b. The person at the bottom of the keyboard (the left-hand side)?

Answer on p. 71

A Pair of Pianos

A duet means there are 16 fingers and 4 thumbs, but only one keyboard.

What if you're at the piano, next to somebody who likes to fling out their elbows?

Maybe you argue about where the middle is.

Pianos are so big that having two in a room is often impossible. So it's a treat to hear two together. The sound is really satisfying.

If you each have a piano of your own, there are no arguments!

You can sit in the middle of your keyboard and do whatever you like with your elbows.

Trimble Buttermilk Point (Reel)

PLAY · TRACK 15 · CD 1 ONLINE PART

The country of Ireland is full of folk music and dancing.

A 'reel' is a springy folk dance with a simple beat.
You step and hop in a pattern. No lazy legs!

Joan Trimble was born in Northern Ireland. Even when she lived in London, she could still hear all this wonderful Irish music in her head. Sometimes she set it free...

Joan had a sister called Valerie. Joan and Valerie played together on two pianos and became famous. They had their own BBC Radio programme for ten years.

Listen...

More and more notes are added around the tune, as if more and more people are getting up to join in the dance. Why don't you join in too!

QUESTION 15

How many pianists are playing the tune right at the start:
a. 3, b. 2, or c. 1
Answer on p. 71

Buttermilk Point was about one of Trimble's favourite places for a picnic!

Keeping Company

A flute playing all on its own is lovely.
No other sound gets in the way.

Like a piece of chocolate, sometimes it's all you want.

But if you put a piece of chocolate in a cake,
you get more flavours.

If you put a flute with a piano, you get more sounds!

You might be really good at playing the piano.
But instead of being in the spotlight,
you can help someone else to shine.

Britten The Plough Boy

PLAY · TRACK · 16 · CD 1 ONLINE PART 1

A piano can make a song more interesting.

And if you're the one singing, it's nicer to have a piano playing too. It helps the notes be in the right places.

In this song, a poor boy working in a field dreams of becoming a great man. You can hear how pleased he is that he will be so important.

Benjamin Britten didn't write the tune of this song – it was there already. But he 'arranged' it to make his own version. It's like giving it a new costume.

Listen...

Listen to the piano bouncing underneath and tinkling on the top, full of energy – the boy is determined to be brilliant!

QUESTION 16

At the very beginning, it is just the piano playing. Then the voice comes in. What happens at the very end?
a. It is just the voice with no piano,
b. It is just the piano with no voice,
or c. It is both together.

Answer on p. 71

Saint-Saëns The Swan from 'The Carnival of the Animals'

PLAY · TRACK · 17 · CD 1 ONLINE PART 1

It's the cello's turn to play with the piano!

Listen...

The cello is the beautiful swan, gliding along. The piano is the rippling water underneath.

QUESTION 17

The music has a melody (a tune). Is the melody played by:
a. The cello,
or b. The piano?

Answer on p. 71

The Carnival of the Animals has other things in it too – an elephant, a cuckoo, kangaroos and even some fossils!

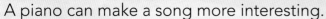

Making Friends

The piano has a lot of friends to play with.
All the other instruments like it.

As well as playing with one other instrument, it plays in groups.
It might be in a trio (three players), with a violin and a cello.
It could be in a quartet (four players), with woodwind instruments.

There are many options.

Each instrument has its own part to play.
The parts go together like pieces in a jigsaw.
They make a colourful piece of music.

Music for small groups is called 'chamber music'. Chamber means room: friends play together in a room at home.

When the players perform the music,
they often look at each other and smile.

Poulenc Trio for oboe, bassoon and piano (movement 3)

PLAY TRACK 18 · CD 1 ONLINE PART 1

Three instruments are playing around in this piece.
Have you never seen a bassoon in the playground?
What about an oboe, chasing a piano?
There are fun and games in this music.

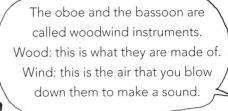

The oboe and the bassoon are called woodwind instruments.
Wood: this is what they are made of.
Wind: this is the air that you blow down them to make a sound.

Listen...

Can you hear the high oboe and the low bassoon?
The oboe has a few notes on its own with the piano at 0.18.
The bassoon answers at 0.22.

QUESTION 18

What happens at 0.56?
a. Somebody starts singing,
b. The oboe squeaks,
or c. The piano has some bouncy notes by itself.

Answer on p. 71

Elgar Piano Quintet (movement 2)

PLAY TRACK 19 · CD 1 ONLINE PART 1

Friends don't always run around together.
Sometimes they sit quietly at the end of a busy day.

And sometimes, music can be so beautiful
that it makes you want to cry.

Listen...

The three instruments swim together
in one lovely pool of sound.

A quintet is for five players.
This one is for two violins, a viola, a cello and a piano.

Elgar was a great British composer.

QUESTION 19

Is there a bassoon in this piece?
a. Yes, or b. No.

Answer on p. 71

33

Screws and Bolts

Shhh!

John Cage was like a scientist in a laboratory. He did experiments with music.

Unlike his name, he wasn't in a cage at all!

He didn't want music to be in a cage either. He wanted it to be free.

John Cage wrote a famous piece called *4'33"*. It was 4 minutes and 33 seconds of complete silence! What on earth did he do that for? He wanted people to listen to the sounds around them. Even if people are completely quiet, there are still sounds. Try it!

John Cage 'prepared' his piano – he got it ready to sound as he wanted it. So it is called 'prepared piano'.

One day, Cage was asked to write some music for the piano. But he got stuck.

'Hmm,' he thought. 'I wish I was allowed to use more instruments.'

He decided that the piano was the problem. He needed to experiment with it.

So he opened the piano lid and put a plate on the strings.

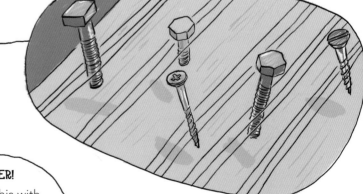

But when he tried to play, the plate bounced around. That wasn't a very good idea.

He didn't give up. He tried screws and bolts on the strings instead – they were just right.

It made the sound completely different!

DANGER!
Don't try this with your own piano – it could ruin it for ever!

Cage Perilous Night No. 6

PLAY TRACK 20 CD 1 ONLINE PART 1

There are many percussion instruments. Drums, xylophones, triangles, wood blocks… even a saucepan can be a piece of percussion!

John Cage loved these different sounds.

With his screws and bolts, he made the piano more like a percussion instrument.

Instead of rich and tuneful, it sounds… spooky.

To 'prepare' the piano, all the bits have to go in the right places. It's complicated!

QUESTION 20

Does this music focus on:
a. Rhythm, or b. Melody?

Answer on p. 71

This piece is called 'Perilous Night'. Perilous means dangerous. The spooky sound is just right for danger.

Listen…

The screws and bolts stop the strings working like normal, so the sound changes. Would you know this was a piano?

Time to Sleep

You snuggle under the covers, put your head on the pillow, close your eyes, and… Oh dear, you're still awake!

Maybe you bounce out of bed but you are told to get back in.

It can take time for your body to switch off.

Music helps your brain to stop buzzing.

The piano can be very soothing.
If you *really* listen, it can charm you like a magic spell.

You start to breathe more slowly.

Your arms and legs feel a bit heavier.

Your eyelids flicker down and don't come up again.

And you're…   asleep.

Maxwell Davies Farewell to Stromness

PLAY
CD 1 ONLINE PART 1
TRACK 21

Stromness, high up in Scotland, has boats and beauty.

It was a very special place for the British composer Peter Maxwell Davies.

Listen...
There is just a simple line at the beginning. When more notes come in, that line carries on underneath. See if you can you hear it.

Composers often write music about a place or a person that is important to them. They can say what they feel in music instead of words.

Satie Gymnopédie No. 1

PLAY TRACK 22 CD / ONLINE PART

Erik Satie was an unusual, quirky man from France.

He wore suits made of velvet, and walked 10 kilometres around Paris every single day.

Listen...

Listen to how still this music is – as if it's suspended in the air. See if you can hear the gentle 1–2–3 swing all the way through – there are three beats in each bar.

Satie wrote some piano pieces called *Three Really Flabby Preludes*. He liked to be different!

Chopin Prelude, Op. 28 No. 7

PLAY TRACK 23 CD / ONLINE PART

Chopin was like a gymnast on the piano. He dazzled everyone with his playing.

He wrote fast, sparkling pieces and gentle, dreamy ones.

He really was a genius.

Chopin came from Poland, lived in Paris and loved the piano. Lots of Ps!

Listen...

A miniature jewel – soft and simple.

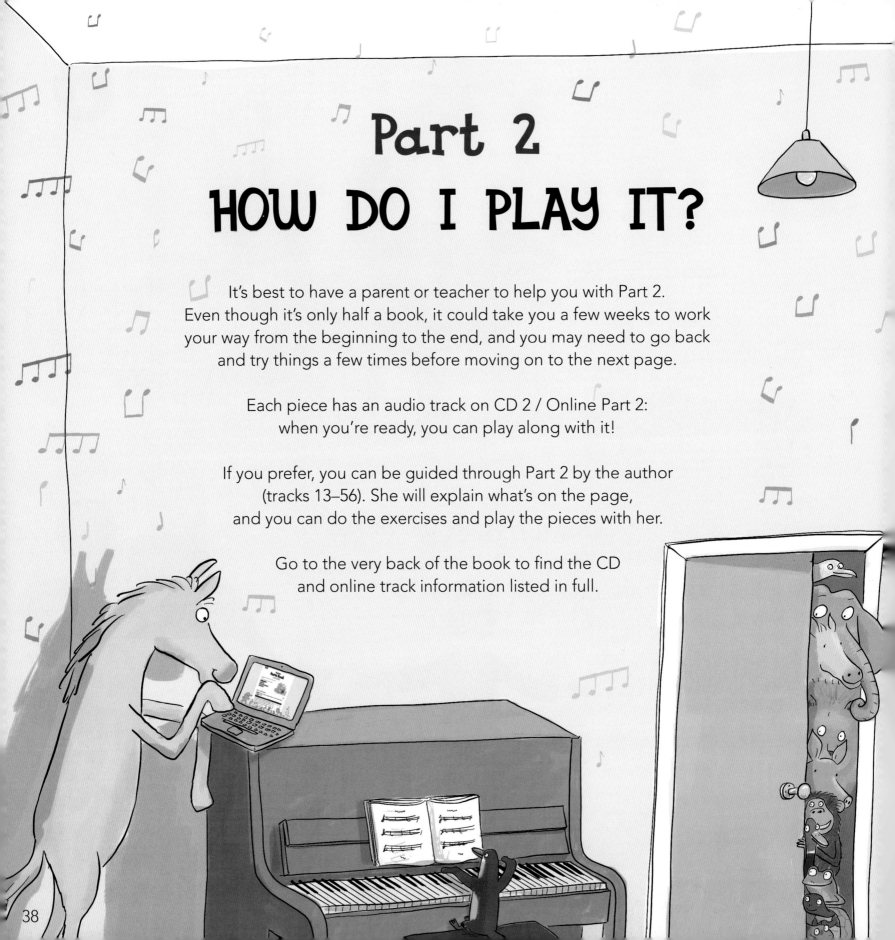

Part 2
HOW DO I PLAY IT?

It's best to have a parent or teacher to help you with Part 2.
Even though it's only half a book, it could take you a few weeks to work
your way from the beginning to the end, and you may need to go back
and try things a few times before moving on to the next page.

Each piece has an audio track on CD 2 / Online Part 2:
when you're ready, you can play along with it!

If you prefer, you can be guided through Part 2 by the author
(tracks 13–56). She will explain what's on the page,
and you can do the exercises and play the pieces with her.

Go to the very back of the book to find the CD
and online track information listed in full.

Sometimes it's hard to believe that the sounds coming from a piano are made by just one person's fingers.

Would you like to be a **pianist**?

This part of the book can help you to get started.

If you play the piano already, you can use Part 2 to see how much you know.

All the pianists playing in Part 1 were beginners once.
They had to start with the basics.
Then they got better and better…

Just look at me now

At first   then…   now!

If you don't have a piano, you can use an electric keyboard.

The UK and the US use different words for some things in music. Here are the ones that we need to know for this book:

UK		US
Bar	=	Measure
Stave	=	Staff
Quaver	=	Eighth note
Crotchet	=	Quarter note
Minim	=	Half note
Semibreve	=	Whole note

Staves and Clefs

 This is a bass clef.

This is a treble clef.

When you see a bass clef, you usually use your left hand. Your left hand is your LOW hand.

Touch your foot with your **left hand** and sing a loud, low note to 'Haw'.

When you see a treble clef, you usually use your right hand. Your right hand is your HIGH hand.

Reach up with your **right hand** and sing a loud, high note to 'Hee'.

Starting with your **right** hand, do three 'Hee-Haws' in a row: reach up with your right hand for 'Hee' and reach down with your left hand for 'Haw'.

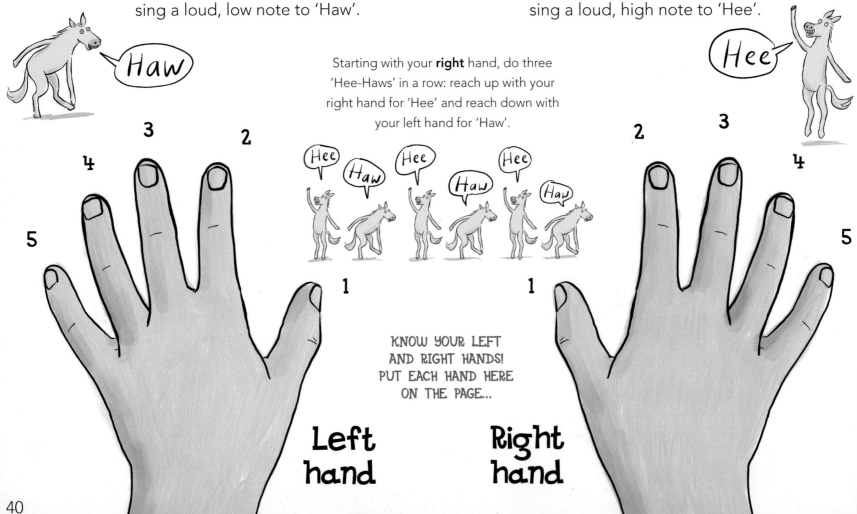

KNOW YOUR LEFT
AND RIGHT HANDS!
PUT EACH HAND HERE
ON THE PAGE...

Left hand

Right hand

40

Clefs don't float around a page wherever they want! They sit on a 5-bar gate called a **stave** or **staff**:

Because the piano has so many keys, the music has two staves joined together: the top one has the treble clef (for higher notes) and the bottom one has the bass clef (for lower notes).

All music notes are written on the lines and in the spaces of these staves. The notes tell you which keys to press and for how long.

The Keyboard

The **keyboard** of the piano has black keys and white keys.

Bottom key - the lowest note

Press the bottom key of your keyboard:
that is the lowest note –
too low to sing!

Top key - the highest note

Press the top key:
that is the highest note –
too *high* to sing!

The piano goes from very low to very high.

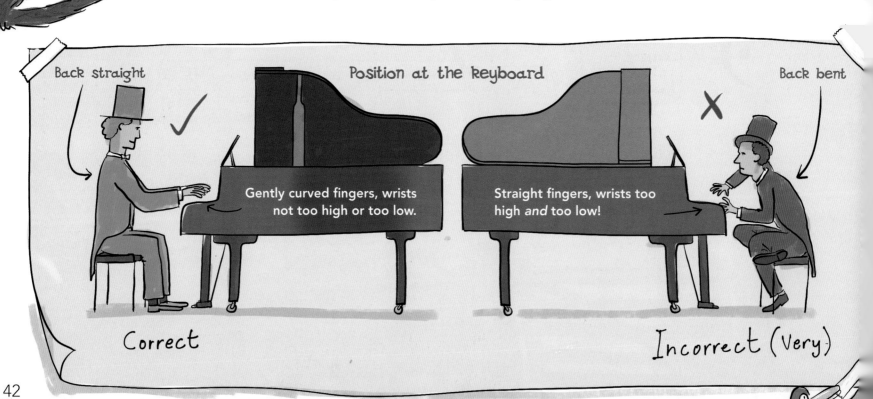

Back straight ✓

Back bent ✗

Position at the keyboard

Gently curved fingers, wrists not too high or too low.

Straight fingers, wrists too high *and* too low!

Correct

Incorrect (Very)

Can You See the C?

There is one special C that we use like an anchor. It is called **Middle C**.
Middle C is near the middle of the keyboard.
Can you see it on *your* keyboard?

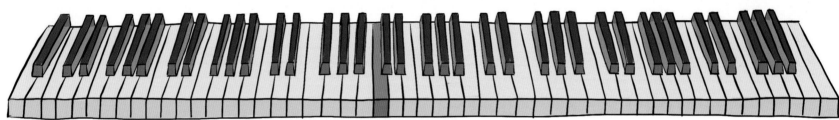

Play **Middle C** with your
left hand when you see this:

Finger marking
- Play it with number 1,
your left thumb

1

Stave,
or
staff

Bass clef
- lower notes for
the left hand

MIDDLE C

Left hand

Play **Middle C** with your
right hand when you see this:

Treble clef
- higher notes for
the right hand

MIDDLE C

Finger marking
- Play it with number 1,
your right thumb

Right hand

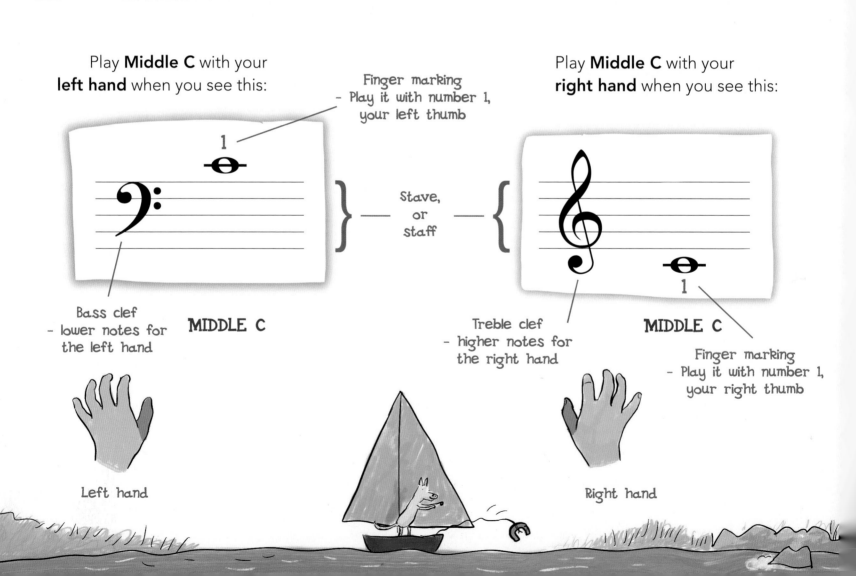

Handy Hint

Try to make sure your hands are in the correct position.

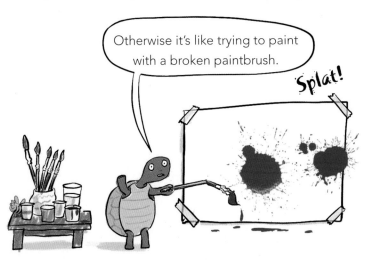

Otherwise it's like trying to paint with a broken paintbrush.

Splat!

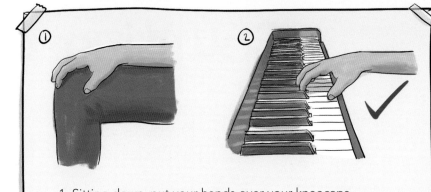

1. Sitting down, put your hands over your kneecaps.
2. Keeping your hands in that same position, bring them up to the keyboard: the tips of your fingers (and the side tips of your thumbs) should be touching the keys.

When you press a key, keep the finger that is pressing it in the same position.
Don't flatten it like a pancake! And don't tighten your hand like a fork.
Keep your hands relaxed and if you forget how they should be, put them back on your kneecaps!

On your piano, find Middle C and play it with the thumb of your **right hand**.

Swap thumbs and play it with the thumb of your **left hand**.

Now try each thumb, one after the other, letting the key come completely up after one note before pressing it down again for the next note:

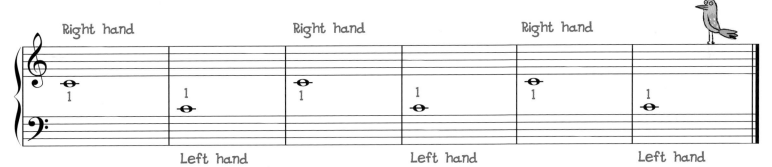

The note of Middle C is where the top and bottom staves meet.
So it has a line all of its own, which floats between the staves.

Try putting on track 1 from Part 1 again:

Middle C is the first note of the piece, and there are a few more Middle Cs after that too – can you play your Middle C whenever you hear them?

45

Counting the Beats

Can you count to 4?
Of course you can!
Do it now, out loud, twice in a row:

1 2 3 4|**1** 2 3 4|

Do it again and clap
at the same time.

clap clap clap clap clap clap clap clap

1 2 3 4|**1** 2 3 4|

Now, instead of clapping, play Middle C – four times with the right thumb then four times with the left thumb.

Sometimes people tap their foot to music: they are tapping the beats. It is beats that help to make **rhythm**, and rhythm brings music alive!

I can count to 4 but clapping has always been a problem

Music is split up into bars or measures using bar lines.

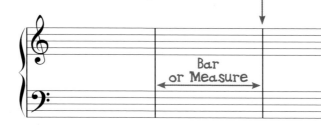

Double bar line: the end!

After the clef – 𝄞 or 𝄢 – you will see two numbers, one on top of the other. This is a **time signature**. For now, just look at the number on the top, which tells you how many **beats** to count in each **bar** or **measure**.

♩ crotchet, or quarter note = 1 beat

♩ minim, or half note = 2 beats

𝅝 semibreve, or whole note = 4 beats

$\frac{2}{4}$ = 2 crotchets / quarter notes in each bar / measure.

$\frac{4}{4}$ = 4 crotchets / quarter notes in each bar / measure.

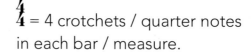

On the piano, you keep your finger down on the key for the full length of the note, even if the sound starts to fade

46

You've now reached the first piece in the book!

Try the piece without the backing track first.
Your goal is to get through it without hesitating or stopping,
so go as slowly as you need to.

When you're ready, select the CD or online track
(it's better if someone can do this for you).

Put your fingers on the keys ready to play.

You will hear two bars of clicks at the start, which match the beats of the bar.
They tell you when to begin and what speed to play –
so try to match your speed to the clicks.

Don't worry if you find the pieces difficult. Just try to follow the notes and play what you can.

Piece 1 Lion

Notes: C

♩ = 1 beat

𝅗𝅥 = 4 beats

WAIT FOR TWO BARS OF 4 CLICKS THEN START

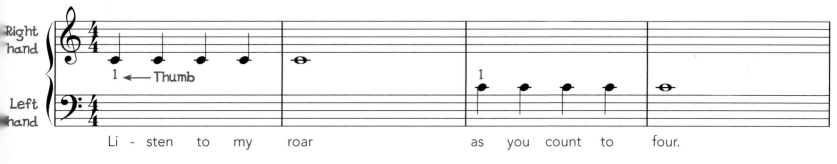

1 ←— Thumb

Li - sten to my roar   as you count to four.

Loud and bold and   proud, I'm told. Come   with me to   ex - plore.

Lions are big and beautiful and strong. Sit up nice and straight when you play.

Sirens

Every white note in between a pair of black notes on the keyboard is called D.

There is a D next to Middle C. Can you find it on your keyboard?

Here it is in the music:

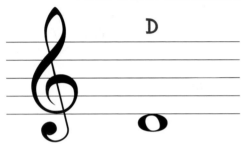

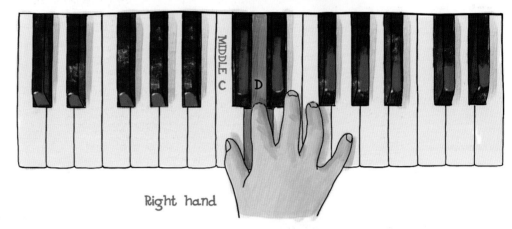

Right hand

Put your **right hand** on the keys with your **second finger** on D. Now see if you can play C and D in turn with your thumb and second finger, like a siren:

Every white note above three black notes grouped together on the keyboard is called B.

There is a B next to Middle C. Can you find it on your keyboard?

Here it is in the music:

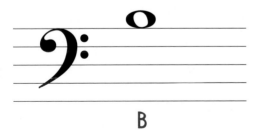

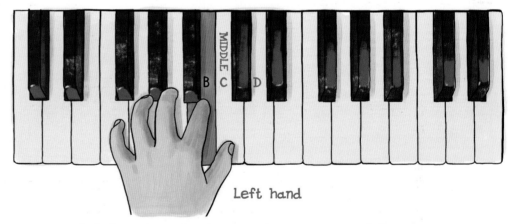

Left hand

Put your **left hand** on the keys with your **second finger** on B. Then see if you can play C and B in turn with your thumb and second finger, like a siren:

Now make a siren with D and B, using both hands:

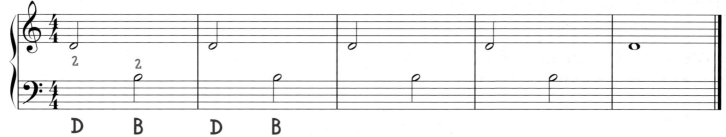

D   B   D   B

Piece 2 Tortoise

Notes: B, C, D

♩ = 2 beats

𝅝 = 4 beats

WAIT FOR TWO BARS OF 4 CLICKS THEN START

Right hand

Left hand

There's   no   point   in   rush - ing   me.

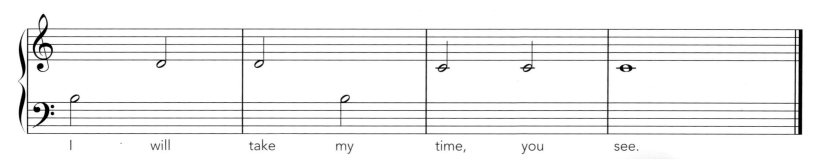

I   will   take   my   time,   you   see.

You can play this one more quietly. The tortoise is shy.

Shhh!

49

E F G

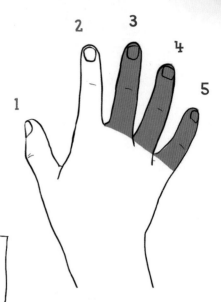

There are three fingers on each hand that haven't played anything yet.

Hold up your right hand and, with your left hand, point to fingers 3, 4 and 5.

note names

Here are the notes for the right hand that you know already. Can you label them?

Right hand

So let's climb up the keyboard and give these other fingers some exercise!

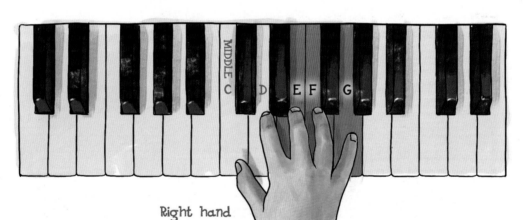

Right hand

Put your **right hand** on the keys and try to find E, F and G with your **3rd, 4th and 5th fingers**. When you find them, play each one in turn.

C   D   E   F   G

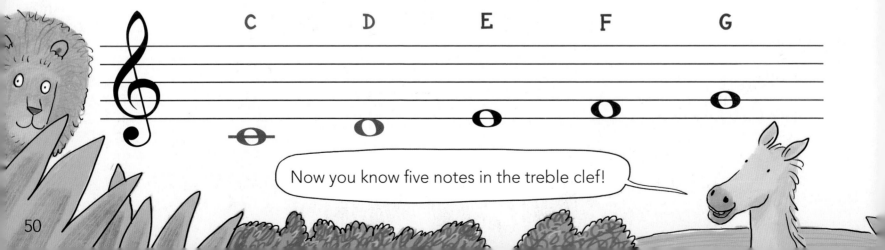

Now you know five notes in the treble clef!

New Rhythm

Clap these rhythms. Clap only on each *note*,
and count the *beats* out loud as you go:

(rhythm notation in 2/4 time)

(rhythm notation in 4/4 time)

But sometimes there are **3** beats in a bar, so each bar adds up to 3 crotchets or quarter notes.

You already know these notes:

♩ = 1 beat

𝅗𝅥 = 2 beats

𝅝 = 4 beats

But what is this? 𝅗𝅥.   This is a dotted minim, or dotted half note.
It is worth 3 beats.
What a difference a little dot can make!

Pieces with 3 beats in a bar often have a kind of gentle swing to them, like a dance.

See if you can clap this rhythm, counting 1 – 2 – 3 out loud as you do it:

(rhythm notation in 3/4 time)

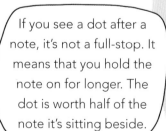

If you see a dot after a note, it's not a full-stop. It means that you hold the note on for longer. The dot is worth half of the note it's sitting beside.

Now try stamping your foot to this rhythm:

(rhythm notation in 3/4 time)

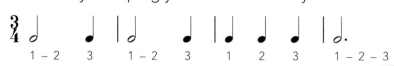

So:

2 + 1 = 3

Remember that the keyboard isn't a trampoline!
Don't let your hand spring up between each note.
Don't let your thumb or finger to play a note,
try to keep your other fingers resting on the other keys.

Piece 4 Seagull

Notes: C, D, E, F, G

♩ = 1 beat
♩. = 3 beats

WAIT FOR TWO BARS OF 3 CLICKS THEN START

Oh   what   a   week,   fly — ing   to   seek

food   that   I   ma — naged   to   drop   from   my   beak.

The seagull is flying high, its wings stretched out,
and a large worm dangling from its beak...

Have a Rest

When you talk, you have little breaks between words and sentences.
If someone replies, you have a bigger break while you listen.

In music, breaks are called rests. They fit with the beats of the bar – symbols tell you how long to rest for:

Crotchet or quarter note rest. Worth 1 beat.

Minim or half note rest. Worth 2 beats.
This little rectangle always sits on the middle line of the stave.

Semibreve or whole note rest. Worth 4 beats –
or a whole bar, whatever time signature.
It looks like the minim / half note rest, except it dangles down
from the fourth line instead of sitting on the middle one.

See if you can clap this rhythm, counting out loud.
Clap *only on a note*: when you see a rest, go 'ssh!'

Now try this one, doing the same thing.

Keep counting 1 – 2 – 3 – 4, 1 – 2 – 3 – 4
carefully all the way through.
Try counting out loud as you play.

PLAY ALONG
TRACK
5
CD 2 ONLINE PART 2

Piece 5 Duck

Notes: C, D, E, F, G

= Rest for 1 beat

= Rest for 2 beats

= Rest for a whole bar

All this flying makes me tired... time for a rest!

RIGHT HAND ONLY

WAIT FOR TWO BARS OF 4 CLICKS THEN START

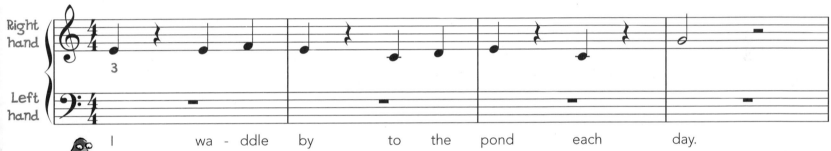

I   wa - ddle   by   to   the   pond   each   day.

Quack,   there   and   back,   pa - ddle,   splash   and   play.

Although ducks waddle slowly, they can lift off and fly through the air!

TA-DA!

55

A G F

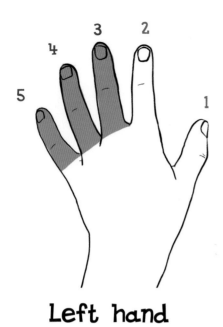

Left hand

It's time for the left hand to play now.

Hold up your left hand and, with your right hand, point to fingers 3, 4 and 5.

Here are the notes for the left hand that you know already. Can you label them?

note
—— names ——

If we climb down the keyboard, these are the notes we find:

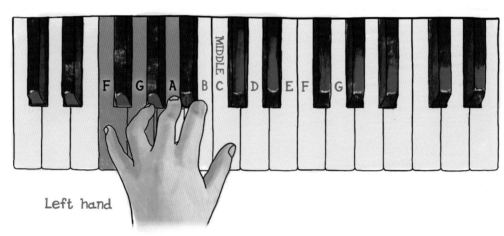

MIDDLE

F G A B C D E F G

Left hand

Put your **left hand** on the keys and try to find A, G and F with your **3rd, 4th and 5th fingers**. When you find them, play each one in turn.

C   B   A   G   F

So now you know five notes in the bass clef!

56

Play them in a row:

Remember!

Remember!

♩ = 1 beat

♩ = 2 beats

1 2 3 4 5

C B A G F

Piece 6 Elephant

Notes: F, G, A, B, C

PLAY ALONG
TRACK
6
CD 2 ONLINE PART 2

LEFT HAND ONLY

WAIT FOR TWO BARS OF 3 CLICKS THEN START

Right hand / Left hand

1 2 3 4 5

Jum - ping   is   not   what   e - le - phants   do.

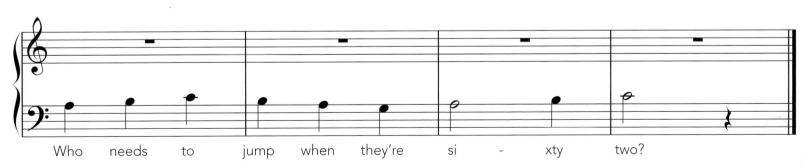

Who   needs   to   jump   when   they're   si - xty   two?

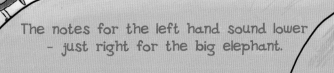

The notes for the left hand sound lower
- just right for the big elephant.

57

Note Revision

So now every finger has played a note on the piano.

Exercise 1 Beginning with the left hand fifth finger, go up the keyboard playing each note in turn with the correct finger – and say the name of each note out loud. You can choose which thumb plays Middle C, or they can both do it!

Left hand

Right hand

Remember the position of your hands. No pancakes!

Exercise 2 Look carefully at this picture.

Playing any notes you like, make up your own piece to match the picture.

BRAVO!

Which animal does the pattern of all the notes remind you of?

HMM, I think I can do this

Exercise 3 Name these notes – each group makes a word. When you have made a word, play it on the piano. *Answers are at the bottom of the page.*

Piece 7 Snake

Notes: F, G, A, B, C, D, E, F, G

SSSSSSSSSSSnake

WAIT FOR TWO BARS OF 2 CLICKS THEN START

Si - lent, I can slip and slide and sli - ther ra - ther well. And

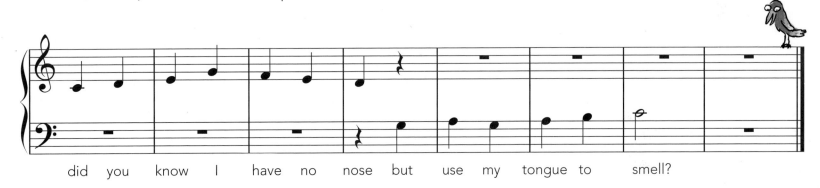

did you know I have no nose but use my tongue to smell?

The move from one note to the next should be really smooth, for the slithery snake!

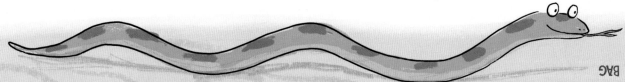

Answers: BAD, FACE, BAG

59

Hands Together

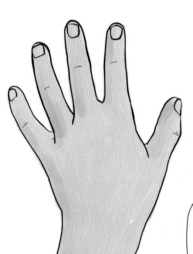

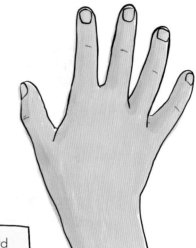

For a lot of things, you use one hand much more than the other: writing, drawing, brushing your teeth.

For other things, you use both hands at the same time: typing, eating with a knife and fork, playing the piano!

It's time to put your hands together. Then you can play notes with both hands at the same time.

Here are two little exercises to start with.

The notes stretch out and come back together again like an elastic band!

Put both hands on the keyboard and play the notes that line up at exactly the same time.

Elastic Band

play Middle C with both thumbs

Bells

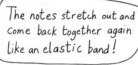

Piece 8 Horse

WAIT FOR TWO BARS OF 4 CLICKS THEN START

Rea - dy, keep stea - dy, pre - par - ing to race,

winn - ing means grinn - ing all o - ver my face!

There was once a race horse called 'Music'. It won only one race!

61

Quavers / Eighth Notes

We have used these so far: ♩ = 1 beat

♩ = 2 beats

♩. = 3 beats

o = 4 beats

Imagine you are walking,
1 beat for each footstep:

♩ ♩ ♩ ♩ ♩ ♩ ♩ ♩

What happens if you start running? What can we write?

We can write this!

♫ ♫ ♫ ♫ ♫ ♫ ♫ ♫

This is a quaver or eighth note: ♪

It is worth **half** a beat.

When there are two, they join tails! ♫

Quaver rests look like little 7s with a blob on. Here: ♪

See if you can clap this rhythm and count out loud.

When you count out loud, 'and' = a quaver beat.

4/4 ♩ ♩ ♩ ♫ ♩ | ♩ ♩ ♩ ♩ | ♩ ♫ ♩ ♩ | ♩ ♫ ♩ ♫ ♩ ‖

1 2 3 and 4   1 2 3 and 4... .

Now see if you can make the frog jump…

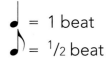

Piece 9 Frog

♩ = 1 beat

♪ = ½ beat

WAIT FOR TWO BARS OF 4 CLICKS THEN START

What a mis-take: I've lost the lake! Hop… stop… I see my way!

I'll make a leap… It's quite steep… Hop, in I plop, hu - rray!

Some frogs can jump over 20 times the length of their own body.
That's a very large leap!

Semitones: B Flat

Look at your keyboard. The distance of sound *between* each key, including the black ones, is called a semitone.

Most of the time, a semitone comes between a white note and a black note. So it's time to learn a black note!

Why was the hedgehog wearing glasses? Because he didn't want to B flat!

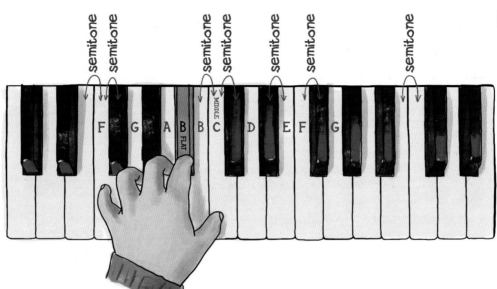

semitone semitone semitone semitone semitone semitone semitone

F G A B C D E F G

'Semi' means 'half'. So semitone means 'half a tone'.

Hmm...I feel a bit flat again

This – ♭ – is called a 'flat'. If you see it next to a note in the music, you play the one immediately *lower*: you 'flatten' the note. This is a B flat:

B flat

Cheer up B flat!

See if you can find this B flat on your keyboard, and play it with the **second finger of your left hand**.

With the **second and third fingers of your left hand**, do a little siren between B flat and A:

2 3

Your fingers can now climb up
an F major scale (like a ladder!) – and down again.

The flat symbol against a note lasts for a whole bar: if that same note is repeated in the bar, it won't have a flat next to it again but you still flatten it.

F Major Scale

Piece 10 Penguin

WAIT FOR TWO BARS OF 3 CLICKS THEN START

Right hand

Left hand

I   wa - ddle   by   and   o - ther   birds   laugh.

Oh   well,   at   least   I'm   not   a   gir - affe.

You can't see its ears, but a penguin has very good hearing.

Semitones: F Sharp

Q: So, what do you do if you see a ♭ sign?
A: You lower the note by one semitone.

If you see *this* sign – ♯ – you do the opposite. It is called a 'sharp' and means that you play the note immediately *higher*: you 'sharpen' the note.

Let's meet two **F sharps**.

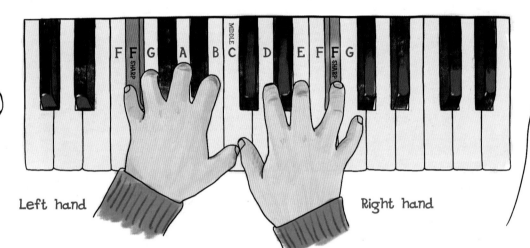

Left hand   Right hand

F sharp

F sharp

Find this F sharp below Middle C with the
5th finger of your left hand and hold down the note...

...then find this F sharp above Middle C
with the **4th finger your right hand**.

Now play the
F sharps one after
the other – like a see-saw!

As with flats, a sharp symbol next to a note lasts for a whole bar: if the same note is repeated, it won't have a sharp next to it again but you still sharpen it.

F Sharp See-Saw

Remember –
still F sharp

Piece 11 Pig

WAIT FOR TWO BARS OF 4 CLICKS THEN START

Right hand

Left hand

Ro - lling in mud is my sort of sport.

Remember –
still F sharp

That's when I do my best grunt and snort.

The film *Babe* is all about a pig. It uses music by Saint-Saëns – with high, tinkling piano sounds.

67

Loud and Soft

Part of what makes music so interesting and exciting is that sometimes it is very soft

and sometimes it's LOUD.

The piano can be soft or loud or anywhere in the middle.
There are usually instructions in the music.
Here are four instructions to learn for the final piece in this book:

Shhh!

Forte, shortened to $\boldsymbol{f}$ = loud

Piano, shortened to $\boldsymbol{p}$ = soft

———————— = getting louder

———————— = getting softer

The words *forte* [for-tay]
and *piano* [pee-ah-no]
are Italian.

The music doesn't change suddenly every time.
So these 'hairpin' markings –

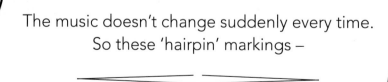

– show you where to change gradually.

Practise with the
Elastic Band exercise!

Elastic Band

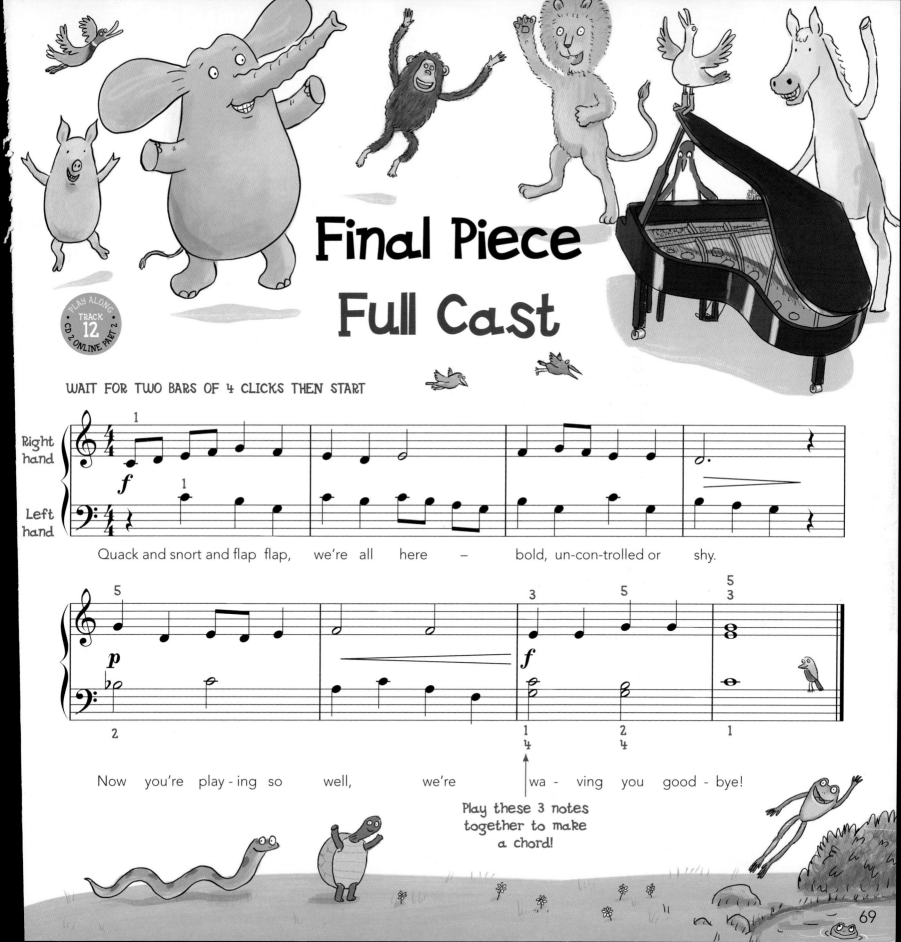

Final Piece
Full Cast

PLAY ALONG · TRACK 12 · CD 2 ONLINE PART 2

WAIT FOR TWO BARS OF 4 CLICKS THEN START

Right hand

Left hand

Quack and snort and flap flap, we're all here – bold, un-con-trolled or shy.

Now you're play-ing so well, we're wa-ving you good-bye!

Play these 3 notes together to make a chord!

Goodbye

This is the end of *My First Piano Book*.

But you can explore much more piano music, here:

www.naxos.com

And if you keep practising, you will get better and better!

At the end of CD 2 / Online Part 2 is one
more piece, by a man called Arvo Pärt.
It is called *Spiegel im Spiegel*, which means
'Mirror in the Mirror'. The reflections go on for ever…

The piano has notes like drops in the water,
and the violin floats calmly.

The style is called minimalism. It uses the same notes again and
again, but there are tiny changes all the way through.

It is hypnotic and peaceful.

Goodbye and happy listening!

Answers

These are the answers to the questions in Part 1.

1. **b.** It keeps going at the same speed.
2. **c.** Just one person is playing this piece.
3. **a.** The melody is at the top, in the right hand.
4. **b.** The music sounds happy.
5. **a.** It ends with the same tune we hear at the beginning.
6. **b.** The orchestra has long, smooth notes between 1.15 and 1.30.
7. **b.** The orchestra plays with no piano at 3.51.
8. **b.** The music is difficult to sing. There's no real tune: the top is a jagged line.
9. **a.** Yes, the pedal is used in this piece. It is very smooth.
10. **c.** The music is bouncy, like the kitten.
11. There is no right or wrong answer. It could make you think of anything… or nothing!
12. **a.** Shostakovich's Prelude is slower.
13. **c.** At 1.26, the main tune comes back.
14. **a.** The person sitting at the top of the keyboard (the right-hand side) is playing the tune.
15. **c.** Just one person is playing – there are only single notes at the start of the piece.
16. **b.** It is just the piano playing at the end of the piece, with no voice singing.
17. **a.** The melody (tune) is played by the cello.
18. **c.** At 0.56, the piano has some bouncy notes by itself.
19. **b.** No, there is no bassoon in this piece. It is for two violins, viola, cello and piano.
20. **a.** The piece has a strong rhythm, but no melody.

About the Author

After a sparkling performance of Shostakovich's Piano Concerto No. 2, Genevieve Helsby graduated with a distinction in piano performance as part of her degree at Durham University. Her passion for conveying the fun and vitality of classical music to children has led to a number of hugely successful books and apps, most notably *Meet the Instruments of the Orchestra!*, *My First Classical Music Book* and *My First Orchestra Book*. As well as teaching the piano, she has presented children's concerts promoting some of these titles, and she recently narrated her own rhyming verses for Saint-Saëns' *Carnival of the Animals* in concert with the Sinfonia of Cambridge.

About the Illustrator

Jason Chapman's busy and varied illustration career has included large-scale illustrations for museums in London, Chicago and Singapore, and long-term associations with the NSPCC, illustrating their Christmas 'Letters from Santa', and Battersea Dogs & Cats Home, illustrating books, publications and merchandise. He has produced many children's books, and illustrated live on TV for the BBC's *Springwatch Unsprung*, after his *Springwatch*-inspired illustrations were spotted on Twitter. Jason's *Stan and Mabel*, about a music-loving dog and cat, was inspired by his previous collaboration with Genevieve Helsby on *My First Classical Music Book*; it was adapted into a hugely successful show performed internationally, including with the London Symphony Orchestra, in Edinburgh with the Scottish Chamber Orchestra, and in Perth, Australia with the West Australian Symphony Orchestra.

Genevieve would like to thank consultant piano teachers Eugenie Aitchison and Sylvia Helsby for their invaluable advice, as well as Sylvie Chalkia for modelling her hands on the keyboard!

Full Track List

PLAY ALONG · TRACK NUMBER · CD 2 ONLINE PART 2

CD 2 / Online Part 2 HOW DO I PLAY IT?

Pieces

All 12 pieces – play along!
Every piece has two bars of clicks before the start.

1	Piece 1: **Lion**	0.50
2	Piece 2: **Tortoise**	0.45
3	Piece 3: **Monkey**	0.35
4	Piece 4: **Seagull**	0.31
5	Piece 5: **Duck**	0.33
6	Piece 6: **Elephant**	0.31
7	Piece 7: **Snake**	0.36
8	Piece 8: **Horse**	0.35
9	Piece 9: **Frog**	0.42
10	Piece 10: **Penguin**	0.28
11	Piece 11: **Pig**	0.35
12	Final Piece: **Full Cast**	0.38

Bonus: Author's Guided Narration

Choose this section if you'd like the author to talk you through Part 2.
You can do the exercises and pieces with her.
Every piece has two bars of counting before the start, and this section includes the sung words.

13	'Hello!'	0.55
14	Page 40: Staves and Clefs	1.29
15	Page 41	0.36
16	Page 42: The Keyboard	0.51
17	Page 43	1.22
18	Page 44: Can You See the C?	1.02
19	Page 45	2.05
20	Page 46: Counting the Beats	2.50
21	Page 47	0.36
22	'So, are you ready…?'	0.38
23	Piece 1: **Lion**	0.55
24	Page 48: Sirens	1.54
25	Page 49	1.03
26	Piece 2: **Tortoise**	0.48
27	Page 50: E F G	0.55
28	Page 51	0.49
29	Piece 3: **Monkey**	0.40
30	Page 52: New Rhythm	2.04
31	Page 53	0.44

32	Piece 4: **Seagull**	0.35
33	Page 54: Have a Rest	1.36
34	Page 55	0.36
35	Piece 5: **Duck**	0.37
36	Page 56: A G F	0.58
37	Page 57	0.58
38	Piece 6: **Elephant**	0.35
39	Page 58: Note Revision	1.08
40	Piece 7: **Snake**	0.38
41	Page 60: Hands Together	1.38
42	Page 61	0.37
43	Piece 8: **Horse**	0.39
44	Page 62: Quavers / Eighth Notes	1.22
45	Page 63	0.32
46	Piece 9: **Frog**	0.45
47	Page 64: Semitones: B Flat	1.35
48	Page 65	1.13
49	Piece 10: **Penguin**	0.31
50	Page 66: Semitones: F Sharp	1.16
51	Page 67	1.16
52	Piece 11: **Pig**	0.38
53	Page 68: Loud and Soft	1.26
54	Page 69	0.53
55	Final Piece: **Full Cast**	0.38
56	'Well, congratulations!'	0.27

To access the audio tracks online:
URL: **naxos-books.com/mfpb**
Password: **penguin**

Goodbye…

57	**Arvo Pärt**: Spiegel im Spiegel (version for violin and piano) – Malin Broman, violin; Simon Crawford-Phillips, piano; 9.70214	8.47

Total: 61.40